T-34-85 Medium 1944–94

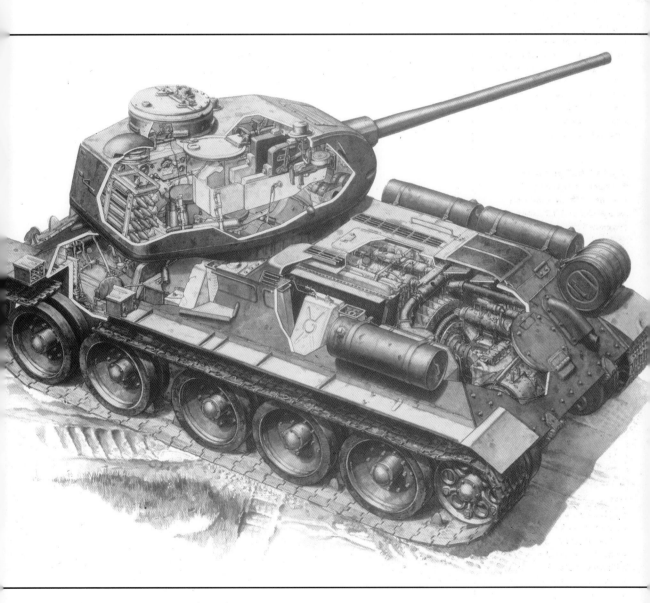

Steven J Zaloga & Jim Kinnear · Illustrated by Peter Sarson

First published in Great Britain in 1996 by
Osprey Publishing, Elms Court,
Chapel Way, Botley, Oxford OX2 9LP
United Kingdom
Email: info@ospreypublishing.com

ISBN 1 85532 535 7

Edited by Iain MacGregor
Designed by Paul Kime
Filmset in Great Britain
Printed in China through World Print Ltd.

Author's Note

We would especially like to thank the following friends for
their kind help during the preparation of this New Vanguard:
first and foremost Janusz Magnuski, the world's most noted
historian of Soviet tank history; Andrei Aksenov and
Aleksandr Koshchavtsev located new material and photos in
Russia. Many other friends have provided photos or other
material, including Stephen 'Cookie' Sewell, Jim Loop,
Simon Dunstan, Karl Rosenlof, Mikhail Baryatinskiy, Just
Probst, Leif Hellstrom, and Russ Vaughan. The text uses
contemporaneous Soviet place names for various cities,
including Gorkiy (now Nizhni Novgorod) and Sverdlovsk
(now Ekaterinburg); these have subsequently returned to
their pre-Revolution names. This book follows the earlier
New Vanguard 9 T-34/76, which the authors' recommend to
readers interested in the earlier history of this tank.

Artist's note

T-34-85 MEDIUM TANK

DESIGN AND DEVELOPMENT

The T-34-85 tank is one of those rare weapons that have remained in service for more than half a century. First introduced in 1944, it has seen combat in nearly every corner of the globe. Although long obsolete in Europe, it has proven a reliable and potent weapon in many Third World conflicts, and is still in service with more than a dozen armies around the world.

As recounted in *New Vanguard 9 T-34-76*, the Soviet defence ministry limited further evolution of the basic T-34 design during the first two years of the Great Patriotic War. Every T-34 was desperately needed at the front and Stalin would not tolerate any interference in the production programme. Modifications, no matter how desirable, would have to wait until the German invasion was halted and the Red Army had successfully counter-attacked in the winter of 1942. When, in

January 1943, the Red Army captured its first German Tiger I heavy tank near Leningrad, it could not fail to be impressed by the thickness of the Tiger's armour and the formidable firepower of its 88 mm main gun. Indeed, its armour was so thick that it was virtually invulnerable to fire from the T-34's 76 mm gun except for close-range side or rear shots. The appearance of the Tiger did not cause major concern to the Red Army at the time as it was not deployed in significant numbers until the summer of 1943. Such complacency was to cost the Russian tankers dearly later in 1943.

T-34, T-43 & T-44 projects

There had been earlier schemes to replace or substantially modernise the T-34. In 1941, two programmes were considered: the T-34M and the heavy T-44 (not to be confused with the 1944 T-44 project). Neither of these programmes went beyond conceptual designs due to the decision to freeze T-34 development in late 1941. In June 1942, with tank production finally reaching desired levels, another programme was initiated. The T-43 was an attempt to create a universal

The first attempt to replace the T-34 was the T-43 universal tank, seen here to the right. This utilised many T-34 components, but was more heavily armoured. Ultimately, the concept proved flawed, what was really needed in 1943 was heavier firepower, not heavier armour.

V. Grabin argued that his S-53 85 mm gun could fit into the standard T-34 Model 1943 turret. Several vehicles were tested in the summer of 1943, but the turret proved too small. This T-34-85 is currently preserved in Perm, but it could be a post-war reconstruction rather than one of the wartime prototypes.

tank combining the thicker armour of heavy tanks within the smaller size of a medium tank. This was paralleled by a similar universal tank, the KV-13, which was an attempt to reduce the size and weight of the standard Red Army heavy tank so as to make it more competitive with the T-34, or its new derivative, the T-43. The universal tank concept proved fundamentally flawed since the focus of attention was on armour protection, not firepower.

The T-43 prototypes became available for trials in March 1943. Aside from its heavier armour – up to 90 mm on the turret – it had other advances, including a new three-man turret patterned after the German configuration. The T-43 shared about 70 per cent of its components with the basic T-34 Model 1943, the main changes being in body design and the new torsion bar suspension. A series of extensive automotive trials were undertaken through the spring.

But at the time of the battle of Kursk in the summer of 1943, Red Army tank units were still based around the T-34 Model 1943, virtually unchanged since the previous summer. The fighting at Kursk revealed the T-34 had finally met its match in the new Panther and Tiger tanks. Both of these new German designs were considerably larger and heavier than the T-34, and far superior in both firepower and armour. Most alarmingly, both tanks were nearly invulnerable to the T-34 during frontal engagements, while the more pow-

erful guns on the German tanks could destroy the T-34 from nearly any practical battle range. By August of 1943, the Red Army's tank force was clamouring for a 'longer arm' – a new tank gun to restore the balance. Earlier demands for greater armour protection were forgotten, and both the T-43 and KV-13 universal tanks were shelved.

Obiekt 135

Although a more potent gun for the T-34 had not been given high priority, the issue had not been completely ignored. After the first encounter with the Tiger tank in January 1943, the Main Artillery Directorate (GAU) had authorised several artillery design bureaus to begin development of a new 85 mm gun for use on armoured vehicles. The bureau headed by F. Petrov at Artillery Plant No. 9 in Sverdlovsk completed a prototype of its 85 mm D-5 gun in June 1943. In the meantime, a team headed by G. Sergeyev of V. Grabin's rival Central Artillery Design Bureau (TsAKB) at Artillery Plant No. 92 in Gorkiy completed the S-53 85 mm guns. These guns were subjected to state trials in July 1943, with the Petrov D-5 winning the competition. The D-5 gun was too large to fit inside a T-34 turret, so it was decided to mount it initially in a special tank destroyer version of the T-34, the SU-85, and in the new IS heavy tank. Although Grabin's design had not won the competition, he convinced the GAU that his gun could be mounted in a standard T-34

Model 1943 turret. A small number of such conversions were undertaken, and firing trials were held at the Gorokhovets proving ground in midsummer. The tests showed that the gun was simply too large for the T-34 turret. Clearance for loading the gun was inadequate, and ammunition stowage was insufficient.

The task of upgunning the T-34 with an 85 mm gun was given very high priority in the wake of the Kursk battles. It was clear from the summer trials that a new turret would be needed to accommodate the 85 mm gun. Due to Grabin's political influence, his gun was selected to arm the T-34 even though the D-5 was already entering production for the SU-85 tank destroyer. To further accelerate the programme, Aleksandr Morozov's T-34 Main Design Bureau (GKB-T-34) in Nizhni Tagil suggested that the project be shifted to the Krasnoye Sormovo Plant No. 112, which was also located in Gorkiy not far from the Grabin bureau. As a result, the Obiekt 135 design was undertaken by a small design team headed by V. Krylov in Gorkiy; the new turret design was assigned to V. Kerichev. The pattern selected was the design already developed for the T-43, but adapted to the T-34 hull. An 85 mm gun was experimentally mounted in the T-43, now called T-43-85. This made it clear that the T-43 turret

Due to problems with the Grabin S-53 85 mm gun, the first production batches of T-34-85 were fitted with the Petrov D-5T 85 mm gun when completed at Gorkiy in February 1944. These are identified from later variants by the distinctive circular housing on the gun mantlet, and the retention of the vehicle radio in the hull.

was not suitable for the new gun without some changes. Aside from adding a neck at the base of the turret to clear the T-34's raised engine deck, the roof layout was rearranged, dropping the gunner's hatch, and moving the commander from the centre rear of the turret to behind the gunner to provide enough space for the 85 mm gun's longer recoil. With the turret design progressing smoothly, in the autumn of 1943 the first set of drawings of the definitive production version of

The 38th Separate Tank Regiment was one of the first units to receive the new T-34-85, their tanks arriving in mid-March 1944 in time to support the 53rd Army during the Umansko-Botoshankakiy Operation. Named after the legendary czar Dimitriy Donskoi, the unit was partially equipped with OT-34 flamethrower tanks. This overhead view shows some of the characteristic features of the T-34-85 with the D-5T gun. The commander's cupola is further forward than on later types, and the gunner retains a periscopic gunsight immediately in front of it.

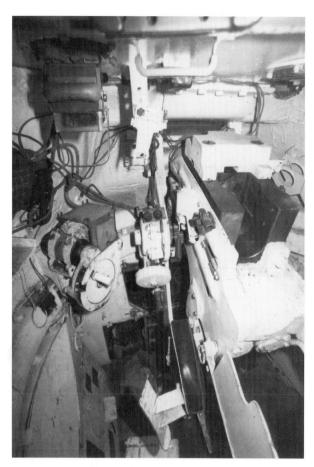

The view from the commander's station (left side of the gun, in this case a ZiS-S-53) inside a T-34-85. Here, the gunner's seat is folded out of the way, but the gun elevation/traverse controls are clearly visible. This museum exhibit lacks the TShU-16 telescopic sight, but the gunner's MK-4 periscope is evident above.

the S-53 gun were delivered to Krasnoye Sormovo. The documents revealed that the Grabin gun was ill-suited to the new turret and was so bulky that it would not have adequate depression or elevation. Grabin was ordered by Moscow to redesign the gun for a better fit. Two prototype T-34 (Obiekt 135) tanks with the new turret were ready in November 1943 and were sent to the armoured forces proving ground at Kubinka near Moscow for firing trials. The testing went so smoothly that Stalin and the State Defence Committee (GKO) accepted the Obiekt 135 for Red Army service on 15 December 1943. It was given the new name T-34-85, despite the fact that trials were incomplete and the design was

not yet finalised. Stalin ordered tank industry officials to have the T-34-85 ready for production by February 1944.

T-34-85 Model 1943

Although the S-53 had already been accepted for production, the normal run of acceptance trials continued, to make certain that it met specifications. During a test in late December, one of the guns failed due to a shortcoming in the design of the recoil system. This created a crisis in the tank industry as several plants were already tooling up to manufacture the new gun and turret. As a short-term solution, the GAU ordered the Krasnoye Sormovo plant to adapt the mature 85 mm D-5S gun to their new T-34-85 turret. This permitted the industry to meet Stalin's deadline, and this interim type, sometimes called T-34-85 Model 1943, was produced at Gorkiy in February-March 1944. In January, the GAU examined four 85 mm guns: Grabin's S-50 and S-53, Petrov's D-5, and the LB-85 from a special GULAG prison design team. The assessment concluded that none of the guns were entirely satisfactory, and that the final gun should incorporate the better features from each. The new head of the Plant No. 92 design team, A. Savin, began to redesign the S-53 using some features from the D-5 and other 85 mm guns. Firing trials in January 1944 made it clear that this composite design was more acceptable than either the D-5 or S-53, and so it was adopted under the designation ZiS-S-53.[1] Manufacture of the ZiS-S-53 began in March 1944 and this gun gradually replaced the D-5 on production lines later in the month. In total, about 800 T-34-85s were built with the interim D-5T gun, and the remainder with the ZiS-S-53.

Design modifications

As the new ZiS-S-53 gun became available, there were concurrent changes in the turret design of the T-34-85. A modified turret was developed by a team under M.A. Nabutovskiy at the main design bureau in Nizhni Tagil. The new gun system replaced the TSh-15 telescope with the new TSh-16 articulated telescopic sight which forced a

1 ZiS is the acronym for Zavod imeni Stalina (factory named for Stalin, the unclassified name for Artillery Plant No. 92 in Gorkiy where the new version was designed).

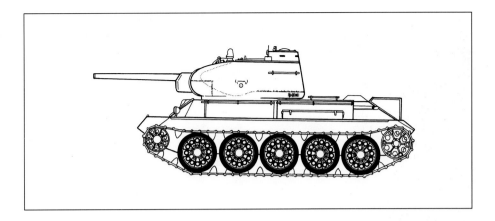

redesign of the interior of the turret, pushing the gunner and commander's stations further towards the rear of the turret. This was evident externally by the shift of the commander's cupola about 40 cm (16 inches) aft on the turret roof. The gunner's periscopic roof sight was deleted and a simple MK-4 periscope substituted. Other turret improvements included the shift of the radio from the right hull front adjacent to the hull machine gunner up into the turret near the commander. This was done to give the commander more convenient control over the radio in combat. The shape of the gun mantlet changed as well due to the method in which the inner mantlet was attached to the new gun, and due to the repositioning of the new telescopic sight.

As several tank plants began to prepare to shift from T-34 to T-34-85 production, the turret casting facilities at Nizhni Tagil and Irkutsk began production of T-34-85 turrets. Different casting techniques at the foundries led to distinct differences in the appearance of the turrets. The most common type, probably produced at the Novo Tagil foundry in Nizhni Tagil, had flattened sides, while the other foundry produced a type from composite castings which was characterised by a sharp joint at the rear floor. The T-34-85 was manufactured at three plants during the war; namely Uralvagonzavod No. 183 in Nizhni Tagil, Krasnoye Sormovo No. 112 in Gorkiy, and the Omsk Tank Plant No. 174. Nizhni Tagil was by far the largest factory, accounting for 78.2 per cent of T-34-85 production; on 26 May 1945 it manufactured its 35,000th T-34. By the end of the war, the T-34 had become the dominant Russian tank. Light tank production had ended in 1943, and production of the IS-2 heavy tank was relatively modest compared to the T-34. In 1942, T-34s accounted for 51 per cent of Soviet tank production; by 1943/44 it had risen to 79 per cent. Ruthless standardisation ensured that the Soviet Union easily surpassed Germany in overall tank production.

Besides the basic gun version of the tank, Nizhni Tagil also produced a small number of flamethrower tanks, designated the OT-34-85. These used the same configuration as the earlier flamethrower on the T-34 Model 1943. The ATO-42 flamethrower was mounted in the right front of the hull in place of the bow MG with stowage of 200 litres of fuel, enough for 30 bursts. Effective range was 70-130 metres depending on the fuel type. This version remained in production in small numbers through 1946.

OPERATIONAL HISTORY

The Red Army began to receive the T-34-85 tank in March 1944. In general, preference was given to Guards formations: among the first units to receive the new type were the 2nd, 6th 10th, and 11th Guards Tank Corps. The aim was to completely re-equip each brigade with T-34-85s, but in fact, many brigades remained mixed formations with both the older T-34 and the newer tank. T-34-85s

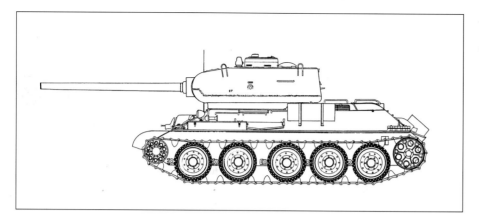

1:76 scale drawing of the T-34-85 Model 1943. (Author)

made their combat debut in late March 1944 during operations in western Ukraine. German troops initially identified them as 'T-43s', a misnomer probably caused when German intelligence learned that the Soviets were working on a modernised version of the T-34, the T-43 universal tank.

This is a rare example of one of the first production vehicles with the ZiS-S-53 85 mm gun produced at Gorkiy in March 1944. The turret casting is identical to the one fitted to the original T-34-85 with the D-5T gun, and still has the inverted U-shaped turret lifting hooks. The design of the gun mantlet was changed for the ZiS-S-53, but the example shown here differs from the standard production item in not having indentations for the attachment bolts. Another feature peculiar to these early production batches is the location of the left side fuel drum. This particular T-34-85 was captured by the Germans during clashes with the 1st Guards Tank Army near the Romanian frontier in April 1944.

Early experiences

In late March 1944, Marshal Zhukov's 1st Ukrainian Front and Marshal Koniev's 2nd Ukrainian Front had nearly trapped the German 1st Panzer Army near Kamenets-Podolskiy on the Ukrainian-Romanian border, sometimes called the 'Battle for the Hube Pocket' after the German commander, Col. Gen. Hube. Field Marshal Erich von Manstein launched a counterblow using SS panzer divisions to help 1st Panzer Army escape. The Soviet tank units had been worn down by the previous month's fighting, 4th Tank Army having only 60 tanks (compared to a normal strength of about 800). T-34-85s were rushed into action to reinforce the depleted Red Army tank brigades. The tankers' reaction to the new design was enthusiastic. Gen. Mikhail Katukov, commander

The T-34-85 Model 1944 was first committed in large numbers during Operation 'Bagration', when the Red Army crushed Army Group Centre, inflicting Germany's worst defeat of the war. This is a T-34-85 of the 25th Guards Tank Brigade, 2nd Guards Tank Corps, entering Minsk shortly after its liberation in early July 1944. The corps insignia is a white arrow, and above it is the brigade letter, a Cyrillic B. This unit was mainly equipped with tanks produced at Nizhni Tagil in March–April 1944. The truck on the left is a GAZ-AA fitted with a captured 2 cm Flak 38 AA gun. (Sovfoto)

of the 1st Tank Army during the fighting recalled: 'During this difficult engagement there were also happy events; the arrival of new replacement tanks was one of them. The army received a new '34, admittedly only a few of them, with the long barrel 85 mm gun instead of the usual 76 mm gun. The crews assigned the new tanks were given two hours to familiarise themselves with the new equipment. We could not allow any more time due to the situation at the front. The new tanks, having much more powerful armament than the old ones, had to be rushed into combat immediately.

The design of the T-34 with powerful new armament infused us with optimism and rein-

forced us psychologically. We could hardly wish for anything more when we saw that the new Soviet tanks exceeded the often praised German tanks in combat capabilities.' The March–April 1944 battles west of Kamenets-Podolskiy were the T-34-85's baptism of fire. The numbers involved were not very large, as the bulk of the new production was being hoarded to rebuild Guards tank corps for the upcoming summer offensives.

T-34-85 versus German Panther
The arrival of the T-34-85 in the spring of 1944 was a welcome relief to Soviet tankers, particularly when it was accompanied at the same time with the arrival of the IS-2 heavy tank. The T-34-85

1:76 scale drawing of the T-34-85 Model 1944. (Author)

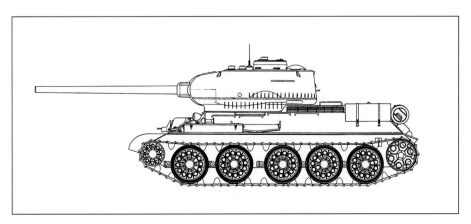

One of the more memorable encounters in the summer of 1944 occurred when this T-34-85 of the 53rd Guards Fastov Tank Brigade, (6th Guards Tank Corps), commanded by Lt A.P. Oskin, encountered a column of new King Tiger tanks near the Polish village of Ogledow. In the ensuing skirmish, Oskin's tank destroyed all three, marking an inauspicious debut for the new German super tank on the Eastern Front. Surrounded by girls from the village, Oskin is the smiling fellow right of the gun mantlet.

did not reverse the German technical advantage in tank armour and firepower, but nearly matched it. The T-34-85 was clearly superior to the most common German tank of the period, the PzKpfw IV Ausf.J, in terms of armour and firepower. But it was not evenly matched against the Panther. This was especially true in a direct frontal engagement, in which the T-34-85 was initially handicapped by standard 85 mm BR-365 ammunition. The T-34-85 could only penetrate the Panther from the sides, or from a lucky hit on the small flat surfaces of the turret face; it could not penetrate the Panther's mantlet or glacis plate. But the Panther could penetrate the T-34-85 frontally at 1200 m against the gun mantlet and turret front, and from 300 m against the glacis. Both the Panther and T-34-85 could obtain penetrations against one another from the sides at 2500 m, the T-34-85 having a slight range advantage against the Panther's weak turret sides. The Panther's prowess was further nullified in the summer of 1944 with the arrival of improved BR-365P hypervelocity armour piercing (HVAP) 85 mm ammunition. This projectile had a special tungsten-carbide core and could penetrate 138 mm of armour at 500 m at 60°, finally giving it the capability of penetrating the Panther frontally.

Soviet success in 1944

A major advantage of the T-34-85 was in numbers. At the end of May 1944, the Wehrmacht had only 304 Panthers on the Eastern Front, the preference having been given to the Western Front in anticipation of the expected Anglo-American invasion. Production of the T-34-85 was running at about 1,200 per month in the spring of 1944. Regardless of whether the T-34-85 was evenly matched against the Panther in June 1944, its gun was more than effective against the PzKpfw IV and StuG III that made up the bulk of the German armoured force on the Eastern Front. By the time of Operation 'Bagration', the Soviet offensive against Army Group Centre in Byelorussia on 22 June 1944, most of the Soviet tank corps had been at least partially re-equipped with the T-34-85, and many units had been almost completely re-equipped.

The T-34-85 played a prominent role in the great victories of the summer of 1944. About 7,200 T-34s had been built in 1944 up to June, of which over 6,000 were the new T-34-85. With the exception of one tank corps, equipped mainly with new American Lend-Lease M4A2 Sherman tanks, nearly all the tank corps participating in Operation 'Bagration' operated the T-34-85. 'Bagration', launched on 22-23 June 1944, managed to largely destroy Army Group Centre in the most crushing defeat of the Wehrmacht in World War 2. The liberation of Byelorussia unhinged German defences in the East and was followed in quick succession by the Lvov-Sandomierz offensive in Ukraine, which put the Red Army into central Poland and Romania. The heaviest tank battles were those around Brody and Lvov during the Ukrainian offensive, where the bulk of the German armour on the Eastern Front was located.

T-34-85 versus German King Tiger

One of the most memorable tank engagements of the war occurred towards the end of the Lvov-Sandomierz offensive in Poland. On the evening of 11 August 1944, Lt. Aleksandr P. Oskin of the 53rd Guards Fastov Tank Brigade (6th Guards Tank Corps) was ordered to patrol the Polish village of Ogledow where he was expected to link up with the unit's 2nd Battalion. The patrol included a team of tank infantry which had been riding on his vehicle through the Byelorussian and Polish fighting since June. On reaching the village, no friendly tanks were located, and German troops were approaching the opposite end of the town. Oskin informed the brigade commander and was told to take up a defensive position and monitor

the German troops. The tank hull was already well camouflaged in a field of corn, and Oskin's crew and the tank infantry camouflaged the turret with corn stalks. A German tank column entered Ogledow that evening and shot it up, but halted after dark. Although Oskin did not know it at the time, the tank unit was a platoon from sPzAbt 501, the first German tank unit on the Eastern Front with Hitler's latest 'wonder weapon', the new King Tiger heavy tank. The unit had disembarked earlier at Kielce with 45 King Tigers but by the time it had reached the vicinity of Ogledow on the evening of 11 August 1944, it was down to only eight tanks. The rest had broken down during the 45 km road march, mainly due to reduction gear failures.

On the morning of 12 August, the King Tiger battalion was ordered into action to help crush the Soviet bridgehead over the Vistula River near Sandomierz. Sitting in his tank, Oskin saw the King Tigers move out of the village. They appeared to be Panthers, but Oskin recalled an intelligence briefing in which the Soviet crews were warned to keep an eye out for a new German heavy tank. In the event, the Germans had not spotted Oskin's well camouflaged tank, and they were moving down a road where their more vulnerable sides would be exposed. Oskin

In mid-October 1944, the 3rd Byelorussian Front took part in the major offensive attempting to break into East Prussia. The attacks were stymied by stiff German resistance with heavy losses, including this T-34-85 of the 25th Guards Tank Brigade, 2nd Guards Tank Corps, the victors in the battle for Minsk only four months earlier. This is a summer production tank and is fitted with the TDP smoke laying system on the rear deck; the MDSh smoke canisters have been detached and lay on the ground.

ordered the loader, A. Khalyshev, to load one of his precious BR-365P hypervelocity rounds. When the King Tigers had closed to 200 m and were broadside, Oskin ordered his gunner, Abubakir Merkhaidorov, to fire. The round hit the turret side of the second tank, seemingly without effect. Actually, it had penetrated and killed some of the crew, but this was not immediately apparent to the Russians. Oskin's tank fired two more BR-365 AP rounds against the turret, and in frustration he finally ordered up another round of sub-calibre ammunition and told the gunner to hit the rear fuel tank. The King Tiger finally began to burn. By this time, the lead King Tiger had begun to swing its massive turret looking for its tormentor, but in all the dust raised by the impacts of the 85 mm gun, they could not find a target. Oskin's tank fired three rounds at the front of the turret, which bounced off without effect. The fourth round penetrated the turret ring, and the lead King Tiger began to burn from an ammunition fire. The third King Tiger, blind in the smoke from the fuel fire on the second King Tiger, began to back off the road at top speed. Oskin

detonated the MDSh smoke cans at the back of his tank to give himself some cover, and began chasing after the third King Tiger. The fleeter T-34-85 soon caught up and Oskin managed to manoeuvre around to the rear of the King Tiger where they knocked it out with a shot into the engine compartment through the thin rear armour. On returning to the road, one of the King Tigers had stopped burning, so Oskin fired at it again with his last round of hypervelocity ammunition. Two of the King Tigers subsequently suffered catastrophic ammunition fires which blew off their turrets. German losses were eleven dead of the fifteen crew including Lt. Karnetzki and Wieman, and some of the survivors were taken prisoner by Oskin's tank riders. The Tiger battalion did not know what had hit them, and their losses were attributed to 'massive anti-tank defences'. The third King Tiger was later recovered and sent to the Red Army tank proving ground at Kubinka, where today it still rests in the armoured force museum. Lt. Oskin was decorated with the highest Red Army award, the Hero of the Soviet Union gold star. One of the popular Russian myths about this battle is that the son of the King Tiger's designer, Ferdinand Porsche, was killed during the engagement.

VARIANTS

The SU-100 tank destroyer

The decision in the autumn of 1943 to re-arm the T-34 tank with the 85 mm gun led to the up-arming of the SU-85. Two different weapons were considered for the new tank destroyer: the new 100 mm D-10 or 122 mm D-25 gun developed for the new IS-2 tank. Both weapons were developed by the F. Petrov design bureau at Artillery Plant No. 9 in Sverdlovsk. The new 100 mm calibre had been selected as 100 mm naval ammunition was already in production. The adaptation of the new guns to the SU-85 was undertaken by L.I. Gorlitskiy's design staff at the neighbouring Uralmashzavod facility in Sverdlovsk. It was found that the larger gun breech of the D-10 and D-25 required additional space inside the fighting compartment. The simplest solution was to move

the vehicle commander's station to the right with a small extension and add a commander's cupola similar to that adopted on the new T-34-85. This configuration was adopted in the spring of 1944 on the SU-85 production line before the new tank destroyer was ready. The main drawback to the new designs was its much reduced ammunition capacity, only 33 100 mm rounds compared to 48 85 mm rounds on the SU-85. Prototypes of both vehicles were completed in the summer of 1944 as the SU-100 and SU-122P. Firing trials revealed that the 122 mm gun was excessive for the T-34 chassis, so the SU-100 with the D-10S gun was selected. Production of the 100 mm D-10 gun began in July 1944, with Sverdlovsk switching from the SU-85 to the SU-100 in September 1944. By the end of the year, about 500 SU-100s had been manufactured, and a further 700 were completed by the middle of 1945. Although some SU-100 were supplied to tank destroyer battalions to replace SU-85s, most were retained in the special new Guards Mechanised Artillery Brigades, formed in December 1944. These were special assignment units designed to be deployed under tank army control to provide defence against the new German heavy tanks such as the King Tiger.

In the later war years, the Red Army adopted the custom of naming tanks after military heroes and prominent figures. This T-34-85 in the suburbs of Berlin in April 1945 is named after the poet Vladimir Mayakovskiy. This vehicle has one of the less common turret castings, unofficially dubbed the 'composite type', since it was made by joining two large castings rather than being a single casting. It is distinguished by the flat rear turret underhang and the lack of the characteristic flattened side of the common turret type.

A T-34-85 tank of the Polish 1st Armoured Brigade on the road to Gdansk on 28 March 1945. This was probably the brigade commander's tank with tactical number 1000, burned out during the fighting at Debogora on 2 April 1945. The white Piast eagle was the standard tactical insignia of the Polish People's Army (LWP). (Janusz Magnuski)

Each brigade was equipped with 65 SU-100s. The SU-100 was first committed to action in large numbers during the January 1945 Vistula-Oder offensive in Poland, and they saw increasing use through the remainder of the war.

Allied T-34-85s

As was the case with the earlier T-34, the T-34-85 was supplied to several armies allied to the USSR in the concluding year of the war. The largest Allied user of the T-34-85 was the Polish People's Army (LWP). The LWP received an early production T-34-85 in May 1944 for training, but did not receive any significant numbers of service tanks until October 1944, when the 1st Armoured Brigade was rebuilt with T-34-85s fol-

lowing the summer fighting for the Studzianki bridgehead south of Warsaw. Five Polish armoured brigades, the 1st, 2nd, 3rd, 4th, and 16th, were equipped at least in part with the T-34-85. They were first committed to action during the January 1945 Vistula-Oder offensive, and saw considerable combat during the closing stages of the Prague operation in May 1945. In total, the LWP received 328 T-34-85 tanks during the war, of which 132 survived the fighting. Plans to deploy an LWP SU-100 tank destroyer regiment were delayed until the summer of 1945.

The Czechoslovak Army deployed the 1st Czechoslovak Tank Brigade on the Eastern Front. In the spring of 1945, while serving with the 4th Ukrainian Front, it was substantially re-equipped with T-34-85s before the Prague operation. It received a total of 52 T-34-85s at the time; by the end of the war it had about 60 T-34-85s.

The Allies formed two Yugoslav tank brigades, which were intended to support Tito's Yugoslav National Liberation Army. Britain formed the 1st Tank Brigade with M3A3 Stuart light tanks in

Italy in July 1944 and this unit later landed on Yugoslavia's Adriatic coast. The Soviet Union formed the 2nd Tank Brigade with T-34-85s and these accompanied the Red Army into Yugoslavia in late 1944.

Besides the Allied forces, several Axis armies employed the T-34-85 in small numbers. The Germans captured a small number of T-34-85s during the summer of 1944, and these were used on an ad hoc basis by some local units. Finland also captured seven T-34-85s that summer, using them against the Red Army until capitulation, and then against the Germans.

LATE-WAR PRODUCTION IMPROVEMENTS

Given the scale of T-34-85 production, minor improvements were inevitable. Most of these changes were incorporated into the design as they became available, and this makes the different variants difficult to distinguish. Aside from cosmetic variations in the turret castings, 1944 saw several changes. An electric power traverse was added inside the turret. The new electric drive

During the battle for the Seelowe Heights on the approaches to Berlin, tankers of the 11th Tank Corps and several other units created improvised anti-panzerfaust screens by taking bed springs from German homes and fastening them to the turret and hull side. The aim was to detonate the panzerfaust warhead before it struck the armour, weakening its penetration power. This T-34-85 of the 36th Tank Brigade, 11th Tank Corps, rests at the foot of the Brandenburg Gate in May 1945 following the capture of Berlin.

took up more space, and as a result, the turret casting had to be changed slightly, accounting for the odd rectangular bulge seen on the left turret side of tanks produced since the summer of 1944. Late in 1944 or early 1945, a new enlarged com-

T-34-85 production

	1944	1945	1946	1947	1948	1949	1950	1951–56	Total
T-34-85									
USSR*	11,050	18,330	5,500	4,600	3,700	900	300	0	44,380
Czechoslovakia*	0	0	0	0	0	0	0	3,185	3,185
Poland	0	0	0	0	0	0	0	1,380	1,380
Yugoslavia	0	0	0	0	0	0	0	7	7
SU-100									
USSR*	500	1,175	1,000	400	1,000	1,000	1,000	1,000	6,175
Czechoslovakia*	0	0	0	0	0	0	0	1,420	1,420
Totals	11,550	19,505	6,500	5,000	4,700	1,900	1,300	6,992	57,447

Soviet production figures for 1946–56 and Czechoslovak figures are based on US intelligence estimates

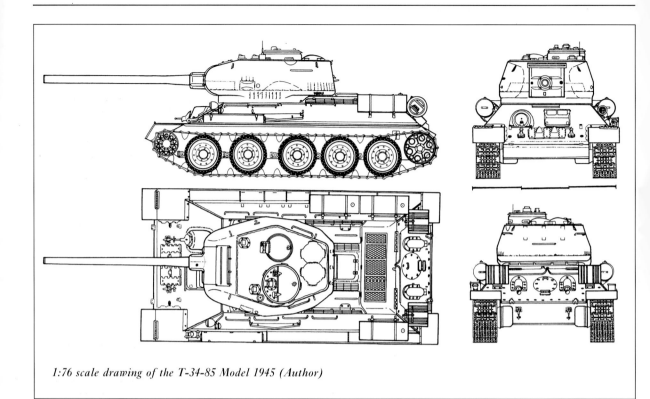

1:76 scale drawing of the T-34-85 Model 1945 (Author)

The lack of armoured transporters in the Red Army meant that tank units carried infantry into combat, clinging to the sides of their tank. This accounts for the large number of hand-holds evident on Soviet tanks during the war. This T-34-85 is entering Budyne in northwestern Bohemia to the cheers of the local Czech inhabitants in May 1945. (CTK)

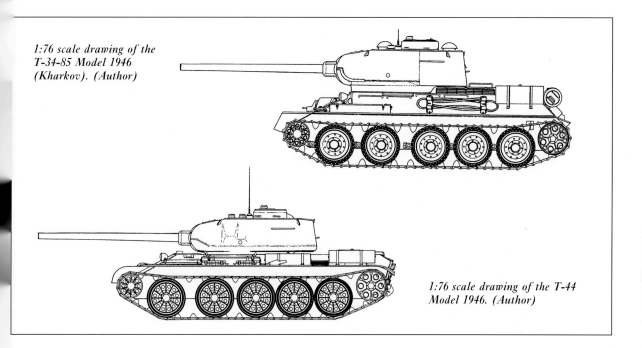

1:76 scale drawing of the T-34-85 Model 1946 (Kharkov). (Author)

1:76 scale drawing of the T-44 Model 1946. (Author)

mander's cupola was introduced which had a one-piece rather than two-piece hatch. On the hull, the tanks produced in the early spring of 1944 retained the rounded mudguards common to the T-34. In the late spring, a simpler front mud-guard with a sharply angled shape was introduced. The TDP smoke concealment system was added to the rear of tanks around this time. The three T-34 plants were supplied with sub-components from many smaller factories and this also affected the appearance of the tank. One of the wheel manufacturers began providing a new cast, spoked wheel which was used alongside the more common drawn concave wheel in use since 1941. Other details changed as well, with the tyre sup-pliers shifting from perforated to solid rubber wheels in 1945. T-34 production in 1944 totalled 14,773 tanks, of which 3,723 were the earlier T-34-76. Total production of the T-34-85 in 1945 was 7,430 through the end of May 1945.

After many encounters with German Panthers during 1944, it was conceded that a more potent gun would be desirable. As a result, several T-34-100 prototypes were built armed with the D-10S 100 mm gun as used on the SU-100. The turret diameter had to be enlarged from 1.6 to 1.7 m to accommodate the gun, and a new, slightly larger turret was designed as well. A few prototypes of

the T-34-100 were tested, but the design was dis-appointing. The Red Army was more interested in the new T-44 and the upgunned T-44-100, so the T-34-100 never entered series production.

In 1944, the Kharkov Tractor Plant No.75, was rebuilt, having been occupied by the Germans through 1943 and later damaged in the battle to retake the city. The T-34 design bureau had been located in Kharkov until the German invasion in 1941, and there were plans to re-establish the plant as the centre of Soviet medium tank design. The factory began turning out T-34-85s in late 1945, making it the fourth plant producing T-34-85s. Around this time, a new turret variant was introduced which split the turret ventilators, plac-ing one forward of the loader's hatch, and leaving only one at the right rear corner. These turrets were used mainly by the Kharkov plant; the stan-dard type of turret casting with the twin mush-room vents was still being produced.

T-34-85 production continued well into the post(cold)-war era. In 1945, limited production of the new T-44 medium tank began at Nizhni Tagil. The T-44 used a turret very similar to the T-34-85, but the hull was an entirely new design featuring torsion bar suspension, a transverse engine configuration and a new transmission. Plagued with teething problems, T-44s trickled

The final tank battles of the war in Europe took place in Czechoslovakia in May 1945. This is a column of T-34-85 tanks of the 16th Armoured Brigade, 2nd Polish Army, identifiable by the brigade insignia, the Polish Piast eagle inside a broken circle. The lead tank's tactical number, 1232, identifies it as belonging to 1st battalion, 2nd company, 3rd platoon, 2nd vehicle. (Janusz Magnuski)

out of the factory while a major redesign was instigated. Not surprisingly, T-34-85s continued to be built in impressive numbers. Developed from the ill-starred T-44, the excellent T-54A finally signalled the end for the T-34-85; in 1950 the last few hundred were assembled at Gorkiy from remaining subcomponents. Including foreign post-war production, a total of 84,070 T-34 tanks were built (35,120 T-34 plus 48,950 T-34-85). Adding 13,170 associated assault guns on the T-34 chassis produces a grand total of 97,240 vehicles. This makes the T-34-85 the most populous tank to emerge from World War 2 and the second most widely produced tank ever. (Its successor, the T-54/T-55, was built in even greater numbers.)

INSIDE THE T-34-85

The T-34-85 was configured in the same fashion as the earlier T-34, with the exception of the turret. As in the T-34, there were two crewmen in the hull: the driver/mechanic and the machine-gunner. On the initial production batch of the T-34-85 with the D-5T gun, the machine gunner operated the radio; in March 1944, the radio was shifted up into the redesigned turret. During much of 1944, there were severe shortages of trained tank crews. The situation grew so desperate that women who worked in the Urals tank plants were enlisted as tank drivers to make up for the shortages.

In addition, it took some time before the tables of organisation were changed to accommodate the fifth crewman needed on the T-34-85. As a result, many tank units only had four crewmen for their T-34-85, and sometimes only three. Generally, the hull MG position was the first position left vacant in the event of crew shortages if a full complement was unavailable.

The turret

The turret contained most of the important changes in the T-34-85. The gunner and tank commander sat on the left side of the turret, and the loader on the right. The gun was mounted slightly asymmetrically to the right to give additional space for the tank fire controls. The gunner sat on a seat attached to the frame of the gun assembly. The commander had a fold-down seat

The Yugoslav 2nd Tank Brigade, formed in the Soviet Union in 1944, accompanied the Red Army into Yugoslavia in 1945. The brigade used the Yugoslav-style star either in red as here or in a white silhouette. This particular tank is fitted with the alternate cast spoked road-wheels.

attached to the turret ring, and the loader had a small saddle attached by snap-ties to enable the seat to be folded out of the way in combat.

Armament

The turret was dominated by the ZiS-S-53 85 mm tank gun. This was a conventional design with recoil recuperators above the gun, a fast-action drop breech, and a barrel length of 54.6 calibres. There were at least three standard rounds for the gun. The standard anti-tank round was the BR-365, a 9.36 kg projectile with a 50 gram high explosive fill. This projectile had an initial muzzle velocity of 792 m/sec and could penetrate 111 mm of armour at 500 m; 102 at 1,000 m and 85 mm at 1,500 m. Later in 1944, the improved high velocity BR-365P appeared (P stood for pod-kaliberniy – subcalibre). This projectile weighed 4.95 kg which included a 620 gram subcalibre tungsten-carbide core. This was a substantially faster projectile, with an initial muzzle velocity of 1,200 m/sec. Penetration at 500 m was 138 mm, and 100 mm at 1,000 m. The scale of issue of this round is not known, but it was probably only a few rounds per tank. The most common round was the O-365 high-explosive-fragmentation projectile which weighed 9.6 kg and had a fill of 775

grams of TNT; maximum effective indirect fire range was 13.3 km. Although much is made of tank-vs-tank fighting in World War 2, tanks more often fired their guns against non-armoured targets, and a good HE round was essential. The ammunition was stored around the tank with 55 rounds being carried; later versions had 60 rounds. There was a rack in the turret bustle that contained 16 rounds, plus four more rounds on the right rear turret side near the gunner. The bulk of the ammunition was contained in the floor in six metal ammunition bins each containing six rounds. There were an additional five rounds stowed in cavities on the right side of the hull. The floor was generally covered with a rubberised mat to protect the ammunition bins. No effort was made to protect the ammunition with wet stowage, as was the American style on the M4 Sherman so as to minimise the risk of internal ammunition fires. A trained crew could usually fire three to four rounds per minute.

The gunner was provided with a TSh-16 telescopic sight, articulated with the gun. The gunner had two sets of gun and turret controls, the turret elevation gear at his right hand and the turret traverse at his left. The first production batches of T-34-85 through the summer of 1944 used a sim-

After the war, many Red Army tanks carried gaudy cele-bratory names and slogans. Here, a tank crew with the Soviet occupation forces in Germany in 1946 listen to tales of past triumphs. The markings on the turret read **Pobeditel Berlina** *– 'Victor of Berlin'. This is probably a tank from 54th Guards Tank Brigade, judging from the painted-over tactical insignia, a '1'0 inside a circle. (I. Kolly)*

ple manual turret traverse system. Later in 1944, an MB-20V electric drive was provided which relieved the gunner of this heavy work during the gun-laying process, and also increased the traverse speed of the turret.

The electric traverse was not precise enough for gun-laying, but was intended mainly to slew the turret into the right position, with fine adjustments being implemented manually. The gunner was provided with a MK-4 periscopic sight over his position, which was used for general observation; it was not used for aiming as was the earlier PTK-5 sight found on the original T-34-85 Model 1943 tanks with the D-5T gun.

New internal layout

The major innovation in the T-34-85 tank layout was the addition of a fifth crewman, which freed the commander from his previous responsibility as loader or gunner. This permitted more refined tank tactics since the commander could now devote his attention to directing his crew and coordinating his tank with neighbouring tanks. This feature alone was one of the most important reasons for the significant improvement in Soviet tank tactical performance in 1944-45, and the higher kill rates against German armour. The Soviet tank designers had planned to incorporate this feature into the T-34M in the autumn of 1941, but had been prevented from doing so by the decision to freeze T-34 development at that time. The Red Army was the last major European army to configure its tanks in this fashion; the Germans had used this turret layout since the PzKpfw III. The T-34-85 commander sat immediately behind the gunner. As on the late production T-34s, he was provided with an all-round vision cupola. This cupola had armoured glass vision slits as well as a MK-4 periscopic sight. The original cupola had a split-hatch configuration; 1945 production vehicles introduced a new one-piece hatch and a larger-diameter cupola. The roof of the cupola traversed, enabling the commander to use the MK-4 periscopic sight in all directions. The second important change in the standard production T-34-85 was the transfer of the tank radio from the machine-gunner's position in the right hull front to the commander's station. By 1944, all Soviet tanks were provided with radios, an essential ingredient in improving tactical handling at small unit level. The T-34-85 was usually fitted with the 9-R transmitter-receiver, an AM radio operating at 4 to 5.6 megacycles with a voice range of up to 24 km.

New improvements

The T-34-85 introduced a variety of other small improvements to the series. The internal fuel capacity of the tank was reduced from 610 to 545 litres, but external fuel capacity was increased from 180 to 270 litres by the use of three cylindrical fuel tanks. In late 1944, the TDP (*tankovoy dymoviy pribor*) smoke system was introduced

A T-34-85 tank serves as the backdrop for a concert by a Red Army unit near their kaserne in Wunsdorf, Germany, in 1946. This is a tank from the 56th Guards Tank Brigade, 7th Guards Tank Corps. The extensive markings on the turret consist of the brigade insignia on the front (O-3), the vehicle tactical number (321) and a red star. On top of this has been painted the battles of the brigade during the war: **Proskurov-Lvov-Sandomierz-Czestochowa-Berlin-Prague.** *On the turret ring is the inscription* **Boevoy put** *(Combat route) 3572 km. (I Kolly)*

which was used to camouflage a tank unit when it encountered enemy anti-tank guns. This consisted of two MDSh smoke canisters fitted to the rear plate of the tank; they were electrically detonated. The mountings for the MDSh canisters were sometimes used for small fuel canisters instead. The T-34-85 introduced improved Multi-cyclone air filters. Later production T-34-85s used the modestly improved V-2-34M diesel engine. The Soviet tank industry gradually improved many sub-components of the T-34 design that substantially improved its durability. For example, average engine life of the V-2 diesel was about 100 motor hours in 1941, but averaged 180-200 hours by 1944; transmission endurance had been extended to about 1,200 km before major repair work was needed.

Post-war western analysis of T-34-85

An analysis of a T-34-85 captured in Korea by the American tank producer Chrysler, conducted in 1951, provides a good assessment of the T-34-85. 'Manufacturing methods had been adequate for the job, with crude exterior finish being countered by precision machining on functioning parts, according to need. Engineering development was actively continued; it was evident that most of the changes had been made to improve tank performance and especially service life, rather than to simplify or reduce costs. Materials were found to be ample for the job – better than those to be used in American tanks in some instances. Design was simple to the degree that the average mechanically trained crewman could attempt repairs with some assurance of success.'

The study found the following negative features about the tank: '[There is] rough steering due to the use of clutch and brake steering control, [and] difficulty in shifting due to the use of a spur gear clash-shift transmission and multi-disc dry-clutch, making driving this tank a difficult and very fatiguing job. There was a rough ride under some conditions, due to an absence of shock absorbers that contributes greatly to crew fatigue as could the excessive noise resulting from the solid mounting of the engine in the hull [no rubber mountings] and the absence of a muffler; all-steel tracks contributed to this. The liquid-cooled engine and its attendant radiators made for greater vulnerability due to the loss of coolant because of concussion, small arms fire or freezing. Wholly inadequate engine intake air cleaners could be expected to allow early engine failure due to dust intake and the resulting abrasive wear. Several hundred miles in very dusty operation would probably be accompanied by severe engine power loss.' The report was also critical of the lack of a turret basket, poor fire fighting equipment, poor

A fine study of a pair of T-34-85 Model 1945 tanks of the Yugoslav Peoples Army (JNA) on parade shortly after the end of the war. Both of these tanks have the common style of turret casting with slightly flattened sides noticeable immediately below the turret handhold. They also have the 1945 production features including the new enlarged commander's cupola with one-piece hatch, and square front fenders.

electrical weatherproofing, lack of an auxiliary generator to keep the batteries charged, and lack of a means to heat engine oil for cold weather starts. The report noted that although Soviet manufacturing techniques were adequate for the job, there were many instances where poor or unskilled workmanship undermined the design, and where overworked machines led to course feeds, severe chatter or tearing of machined surfaces, a consequence no doubt of the extreme pressures placed on plants to ensure maximum output. For example, in the tank inspected (manufactured in 1945) the soldering job on the radiator was so poor that it effectively lost half of its capacity. Soviet tank design philosophy was clearly oriented towards providing a low-cost, durable design with no frills. These pragmatic choices meant that the Soviet Union was able to substantially out produce Germany in tanks throughout the war, even though its industrial base was considerably weaker due to the huge factory losses in 1941. The success of her industry in World War 2 was instrumental in delivering victory for the Soviet Union.

Foreign T-34-85 production

In the early 1950s, after East-Central Europe had fallen under Soviet control, the USSR began a programme to reorganise the satellite armies along a Soviet pattern. One aspect of this programme was to modernise the Warsaw Pact armies with new equipment, much of it to be produced locally. The only two countries in the region with sufficient industrial capacity to manufacture tanks

In the autumn of 1946, one of the turret foundries began producing modified turrets with two separate mushroom domes on the roof instead of two joined together on the rear of the turret roof as previously. This is an example of such a turret on a T-34-85 on parade in Moscow. This type of turret was used by at least two Soviet tank plants, including Kharkov.

were Poland and Czechoslovakia. In Poland, the Bumar Plant in Labedy was selected for tank assembly. Although not the most modern tank, licence production rights for the T-34-85 were sold to Poland. The first tanks were completed in 1951, and production continued until 1955, when the T-54A came on stream. Polish vehicles represented the definitive production version of the T-34-85. Although similar in most respects to their Soviet counterparts, Polish T-34-85s can usually be distinguished by their considerably smoother turret castings. Polish T-34-85s were also sold to some of the other Warsaw Pact states including East Germany.

Czechoslovakia began to undertake T-34-85 production at the same time as Poland. A new factory was erected at Martin, in Slovakia, for final assembly. Czechoslovak T-34-85s closely resembled the Polish tanks in basic configuration, and likewise had a more refined turret casting. Czechoslovak tanks can be distinguished from the Polish vehicles by the housing for an infantry signal button on the rear corner of the left hull side, and by the use of the post-war pattern tow-cable assembly on the left hull side. The Stalin Plant in Martin also began licence production of the related SU-100 at the same time. Czechoslovak

production of the T-34-85 was considerably greater than in Poland, in part due to a later start in T-54A production, but also because the Soviet Union authorised the Czechoslovak government to export its weaponry to the Mid-East in the early 1950s. The most important of these sales was to Egypt in 1956, which involved several hundred T-34-85 and SU-100 tank destroyers. T-34-85 production in Czechoslovakia lasted until 1958 when T-54A production began.

Yugoslavia considered licence manufacture of the T-34-85 in the late 1940s. But it was decided to introduce a variety of changes before production began, and the tank was renamed as the Teski Tenk Vozilo A (Heavy Tank Type A). These changes included a new, locally designed turret and a modified hull with the front corners of the superstructure angled. Seven prototypes were built in 1949-50, but the effort collapsed when Soviet

A T-34-85 Model 1946 of the 2nd Taman Guards Rifle Division on parade in Moscow's Red Square on 'Tankman's Day', 8 September 1946. This is a post-war production vehicle with the modified turret with split mushroom vents, the new solid tyre road-wheels, and the enlarged commander's cupola. It also has several other features seen only on post-war tanks such as the tow-cable stowed on the hull side in front of the fuel canisters. (Batanov)

support was withdrawn after relations between Stalin and Tito soured.

POST-WAR MODIFICATIONS

Although the T-34-85 was becoming obsolete by the 1960s, there were a number of modernisation programmes. These tanks did not usually serve in front-line Warsaw Pact units, but they remained a staple of reserve formations for over a decade. The Soviet Union had two major modernisation programmes for the T-34-85. The first of these began in 1960. The V-2-34 engine was replaced by the improved V-34-M11 with the new VTI-3 air-cleaners, and other small modifications were made to the cooling and lubrication system. A GT-4563A or G-731 generator was added to keep the batteries charged. The TDP tank smoke system at the rear of the vehicle had the new BDSh canisters fitted in place of the wartime MDSh types. The driver's station had a BVN infra-red driving sight installed, and an FG-100 infra-red headlight was added next to the normal white light headlight for night driving. The wartime 9-R radio was replaced by the improved 10-RT-26E. Modifications introduced on the T-34-85 Model 1960 were also undertaken on related vehicles such as the SU-100. Similar programmes were also instituted in Poland, Czechoslovakia and the other Warsaw Pact countries. The upgraded Polish tanks were designated T-34-85M1.

A second modernisation programme was instituted in 1969. This was not as extensive as in 1960, but it was a cheap and effective way of making these old tanks more compatible with the current Soviet supply network.

Older components such as the 10-RT radio were replaced by the latest R-123. The infra-red night driving equipment was replaced with newer periscopes and headlights, and some small automotive upgrades were undertaken. Externally, a fuel pump and its associated stowage box were added to the left hull side to make it easier to obtain fuel from the external tanks. The two BDSh smoke discharger racks were usually removed, or repositioned on the left hull side between the fuel pump box and the external fuel cell. Its replacement was a new pair of stowage racks which could be used to carry a 200-litre fuel drum and an unditching beam.

In the 1970s, a new replacement wheel was developed for the T-34-85 and T-44 that resembled the T-55 starfish wheel, although it had a narrower track. Not all T-34-85 Model 1969 received this new wheel; it was added only when existing stocks of the older wheels were exhausted at local rebuilding plants.

The Warsaw Pact countries also introduced some of these changes on their T-34-85s, though this was not done uniformly. Poland made more extensive efforts to modernise its T-34-85s than Czechoslovakia, as the T-34-85 remained a more important element of its inventory. This version,

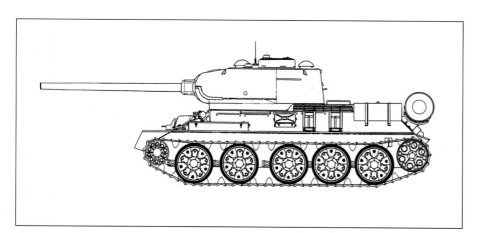

1:76 scale drawing of the T-34-85 Model 1969. (Author)

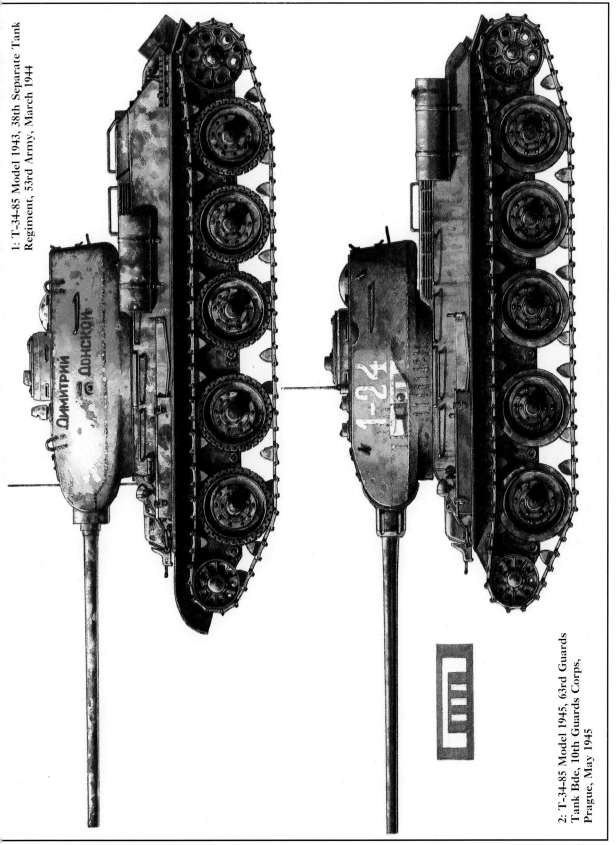

1: T-34-85 Model 1943, 38th Separate Tank Regiment, 53rd Army, March 1944

2: T-34-85 Model 1945, 63rd Guards Tank Bde, 10th Guards Corps, Prague, May 1945

A

1: T-34-85 Model 1944, 55th Guards Tank Bde, 7th Guards
Tank Corps, Berlin 1945

B

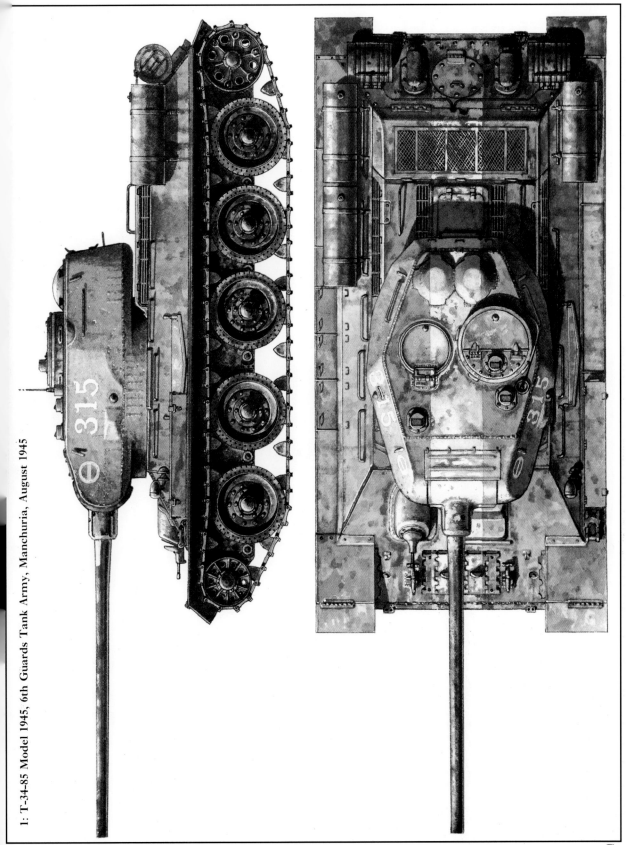

1: T-34-85 Model 1945, 6th Guards Tank Army, Manchuria, August 1945

C

T-34-85 MODEL 1945

105th Armoured Brigade, North Korean People's Army, Seoul, South Korea, July 1950

SPECIFICATIONS

Crew: Five
Combat weight: 32 metric tons
Power-to-weight ratio: 14.2 hp/T
Hull length: 6.1m
Overall length: 8.1m
Width: 3.0m
Engine: V-2-34 diesel, 4-stroke, 12 cylinder, 500 hp @ 1,800 rpm
Transmission: dry multiplate clutch, mechanical gearbox, one stage side drives with side clutches and strap brakes, 4 forward, 1 reverse gears
Fuel capacity: 545 litres internal; 270 litres external
Max. speed (road): 55 km/h
Max. speed (cross-country): 30 km/h
Max. range: 300 km (road)
Fuel consumption: 2.7 litres/km
Fording depth: 1.3m
Armament: 85mm ZiS-S-53 85mm gun (54.6 calibres long)
Main gun ammunition: BR-365 armour piercing; BR-365P sub-calibre armour piercing; OF-365 high explosive/ fragmentation
Muzzle velocity: 1,200 m/s (BR-365P)
Max. effective range: 13.3 km (HE indirect fire)
Stowed main gun rounds: 55-60
Gun depression/ elevation: -5 to +25 degrees
Secondary armament: hull mounted and co-axial DTM 7.62mm machine gun
Armour: 90mm (turret front); 75mm (turret side); 75mm (turret rear); 47mm (hull glacis); 60mm (hull side); 47mm (hull rear)

KEY

1. Tow hook
2. Spare track unit
3. Foot brake
4. Driving lever
5. Escape hatch
6. Hooks for rear turret stowage
7. Rear turret ammunition stowage
8. Turret ventilation fan
9. Amoured ventilator cover
10. Commander's view port
11. Tank radio transceiver
12. Commander's intercom control
13. Commander's traversible hatch
14. Commander's Mk-4 periscope
15. Commander's folding seat
16. Gun shell catch
17. Loader's hatch
18. Loader's ready ammunition stowage
19. Gun counter weight
20. Gunner's telescopic sight
21. 85mm gun breech
22. Gunner's seat
23. Loader's Mk-4 periscope
24. Gun breech lever
25. Loader's seat
26. Co-axial 7.62mm DT machine gun
27. Spare 7.62mm machine gun ammunition
28. Pistol port tampon
29. External fuel tank
30. V-2 diesel engine
31. Air filter
32. Engine compartment fan
33. Armoured louvres
34. Exhaust pipe
35. Engine starter
36. Electrical conduit for smoke cannisters
37. Smoke cannister
38. Transmission
39. Transmission brake drums
40. Drive sprocket
41. Road wheel
42. Engine radiator
43. Internal fuel cell
44. Spring suspension
45. Vehicle saw
46. Internal fuel cell
47. Rubber floor mat
48. Floor ammunition bins
49. Driver's seat
50. ZIP (tool) box
51. Idler wheel

T-34-85 Model 1953 (Czech production), 44th Armoured Bde, Syrian Army, Golan Heights, June 1967

E

T-34-85 Model 1960 (Czech production), Lebanese Civil War, Beirut, 1982

F

1: T-34 (122mm D-30) Self-propelled Howitzer, Syrian Army, Golan Heights, 1973

2: T-122 (122mm Self-propelled Howitzer), Egyptian Army, 1980

Post-war, remaining T-34-85s in the Red Army were put through two major rebuilds, resulting in the Model 1960 and Model 1969 variants. This is a T-34-85 Model 1969. Some rebuilds include the reinforced mounting for the external fuel tanks, the new starfish wheels, and the infra-red driver's headlight on the left side, with the white light searchlight sometimes moved to the right side. This tank has a post-war composite turret with split mushroom vents.

called the T-34-85M2, was the most extensively modernised of all T-34-85s. It included additions on the outside of the vehicle for stowage, a water-proofing kit to permit deep-wading, associated snorkel equipment, and other features. Some countries added their own local modifications. For example, Bulgaria replaced the loader's hatch with a local type fitted with a traversable external anti-aircraft MG.

TECHNICAL SUPPORT VARIANTS

With the T-34 becoming increasingly obsolete, the Soviet Army began rebuilding many chassis as technical support vehicles. The simplest of these conversions involved the removal of the turret, and the substitution of a simple sheet of steel over the turret ring with a hatch or a cupola. Some of these conversions were undertaken by workshops during World War 2, but they did not become common until after the war when a formal pro-gramme began. These turretless tractors were called T-34-T (T = *tyagach*, tractor). In 1955 a

more elaborate support vehicle was developed, the SPK-5 self-propelled crane. This was a turretless T-34 fitted with a crane for lifting up to 10 tonnes. These were used in tank repair units to lift heavy components such as engines and trans-missions. These were later upgraded as the SPK-5/10M which introduced hydraulic and electrical power assist to the crane. Finally, in 1958, the most elaborate of the technical support vehicles was developed, the T-34-TO (TO = *tekhnicheskoe obsluzhivanie*, technical maintenance). This type had an extensive array of tools and repair equip-ment added, and is distinguishable by a work plat-form mounted over the engine deck. There were also a large number of locally improvised demili-tarised support vehicles built by civilian firms for heavy construction, logging and other non-military applications.

Both Poland and Czechoslovakia manufactured their own recovery versions of the T-34-85. The Czechoslovaks were the only ones to actually man-ufacture these vehicles rather than convert old examples. This recovery vehicle, designated VT-34, had a large fixed superstructure in the front housing two crew men and a large 30 ton winch. The layout of the VT-34 was clearly influenced by the Bergepanther, and the entrenching spade at the rear of the vehicle is obviously based on the German design. The VT-34 served as the basis for a Polish derivative, designated CW-34. In the

1960s, the Poles began converting obsolete SU-85, SU-100 and T-34-85s into the WPT-34 repair and maintenance vehicle. The WPT-34 had a crane to assist in field repairs. The East German NVA built its own recovery vehicle, a cross between the VT-34 and the Soviet T-34-TO, which had an externally mounted winch over the turret race. Both the Poles and the Czechs experimented with heavy crane versions of the T-34, but these were never produced in large numbers.

The Czechoslovak army was unique in deploying an armoured bridgelayer based on the T-34-85. Work on this began in 1951 at CKD Sokolovo using the new PM-34 scissors bridge. The resulting vehicle was designated MT-34 (mostny tank = bridging tank). A small number of T-34-85s were converted for this role at the Novy Jicin tank repair facility in the late 1950s.

Countries employing the T-34-85

Warsaw Pact	Mid-East	Africa
Bulgaria*	Egypt*	Algeria*
Czechoslovakia	Iraq	Angola*
Germany (DDR)	Lebanon*	Congo*
Hungary	Libya*	Equatorial Guinea*
Poland	Syria*	Ethiopia*
Romania*	Yemen (YAR)	Guinea*
USSR	Yemen (PDRY)*	Guinea-Bissau*
		Mali*
Europe	**Asia-Pacific**	Mozambique*
Albania*	Afghanistan*	Somalia*
Austria	China (PRC)*	Sudan*
Cyprus	Korea (DPRK)*	Togo*
Finland	Laos	Zimbabwe*
Yugoslavia*	Mongolia*	
	Vietnam*	**Other**
		Cuba

In service in 1996

T-34-85 IN POST-WAR COMBAT

Given the sheer numbers of T-34-85s manufactured, it is not surprising that they have been sold or supplied to more than 30 different states. The list above indicates which countries are known to have employed the T-34-85. Surprisingly, more than 20 armies still employ the T-34-85, though many are in war reserves or on the verge of retirement; those still using the T-34-85 in the 1990s are indicated with an asterisk. Active users of the T-34-85 are not confined to the developing world. Even in 1990, after the Warsaw Pact collapsed, the Romanian Army still had 1,060 T-34-85s and 84 SU-100s in service; Bulgaria had 670 T-34-85s and 173 SU-100s; and Hungary had 72 T-34-85s. The T-34-85 has also been provided to several guerrilla movements including the Polisario and PLO which have used them in combat. Several armies have captured the T-34-85 in combat, including Israel and South Africa, but do not appear to have integrated them into their own armed forces.

The Korean War

Nowhere was the combat employment of the T-34-85 more pivotal than in the Korean conflict in 1950. When the North Korean People's Army (NKPA) invaded in June 1950, the T-34-85 gave them an unparalleled offensive capability in a region where armoured vehicles were rare. While puny by today's standards, in 1950 the North Korean tank force was the most powerful in Asia except for the Red Army. The US Army had only a few companies of M24 Chaffee light tanks in Japan, and China's armoured force was a motley collection of a few dozen captured Japanese and American tanks. The 105th Armoured Brigade received its full complement of T-34-85 tanks in October 1949; each of its three regiments was equipped with 40 T-34-85 tanks. At the time of the 1950 invasion, the NKPA possessed 258 T-34-85 tanks: about half in the 105th Armoured Brigade; the remainder in a variety of regiments and battalions still being organised.

The North Korean Army used the 105th Armoured Brigade as the spearhead of its invasion of South Korea. As Korea is an extremely mountainous country, the brigade did not fight as a single unit, its regiments being doled out to support lead NKPA infantry divisions. The 109th Tank Regiment, attached to the NKPA 3rd Infantry Division, led the attack at 0500 hours on 25 June 1950 near Sachang-ni in the westernmost section

The successor to the T-34-85 was the T-44 medium tank. The turret of the T-44 bears many similarities to the T-34-85, though in fact it is substantially different in many details. This is a rebuilt T-44M preserved at the World War 2 memorial at Poklonna hills southwest of Moscow. It still retains the original narrow tracks, but has been rebuilt with the 1969 starfish wheels.

of South Korea. This unit overran the Republic of Korea (ROK) 17th Infantry Regiment. The 203rd Tank Regiment supported the 1st Infantry Division during its attack along the Kaesong-Seoul 'Unification' highway, and overran the ROK 12th Regt. of the 1st Infantry Div. at Kaesong and the 13th Regt. near a ford over the Imjin river near Korangpo. The 107th Tank Regiment, supporting the NKPA 4th Infantry Division, crushed several units of the ROK 7th Infantry Division along the Yonchon-Seoul road. The South Korean troops had never practiced defence against tanks, and the miserable performance of their 57 mm guns and 2.36 inch bazookas was demoralisng. In desperation, several Korean infantry units attempted to stop enemy tanks with improvised satchel charges or TNT blocks wrapped around grenades. The helplessness of the South Korean infantry led to 'tank panic', fatally weakening the ROK's defences.

On 5 July, the NKPA made contact with newly arrived American troops, when 33 T-34-85 tanks of the 107th Tank Regiment engaged elements of Task Force Smith of the 24th Infantry Division near Osan. Artillery and bazookas proved ineffective and Task Force Smith was mauled. In July, the 105th Armoured Brigade was given the honorary title of 105th Seoul Tank Division for its

To provide additional room inside the fighting compartment compared to the original SU-85 tank destroyer, the SU-100 superstructure incorporated this extension under the commander's cupola. This SU-100 at the Polish tank officer school in Poznan is from the wartime production batches, and lacks the large stowage bin later fitted on the front right corner of the superstructure. (Janusz Magnuski)

An SU-100 Model 1969 takes part in the May 1990 Victory Day celebrations in Moscow commemorating the 45th anniversary of the war. This appears to be an SU-100 built during the war, but it features the Model 1969 upgrades including the starfish wheels, fuel pump external stowage box and the infra-red driver's headlight.

The SU-100 Model 1969 still serves in several armies, including the Romanian Army as seen here. This vehicle shows many of the Model 1969 refits, including the fuel pump box and cable assembly on the superstructure side, and the new stowage racks for 200-litre fuel drums on the hull rear.

central role in the North Korean victory. The NKPA continued to push south towards the Pusan perimeter where US troops were arriving.

The first tank-vs-tank fighting took place near Chonjui on 10 July when the M24 light tanks of Co. A, 78th Tank Battalion, supporting the 24th Infantry Division, encountered NKPA T-34-85s. They scored several direct hits, but the M24's 75 mm gun could not penetrate the frontal armour of the T-34-85. Only two of the original 14 tanks of

the company survived the first few weeks of combat and two other M24 tank companies were also decimated. US Army commanders soon lost confidence in tank support and pleaded instead for better anti-tank weapons. Supplies of 3.5 inch 'super-bazookas' were airlifted to Korea in mid-July.

The US Army 24th Infantry Division put them into use for the first time at Taejon on 20 July. To convince his troops that the new bazookas could destroy the previously invulnerable T-34, the divisional commander, Maj. Gen. William F. Dean, took personal command of a tank-hunting team through the streets of the town. The NKPA lost about 15 tanks in the fighting for Taejon, their heaviest armoured losses to date. Although bloodied, the NKPA took the town in no small measure due to their effective use of tanks. On 23 July several more T-34-85s were destroyed in minefields and by bazookas during a bloody battle with the 'Wolfhounds' of the 27th Infantry at Kumchon, the first time an NKPA armoured attack had been stopped by US infantry. By August, the 105th Armoured Brigade had lost its momentum after being reduced in strength to about 40 tanks from battlefield encounters, increasingly damaging UN air attacks and mechanical breakdowns.

US Army and Marine tank battalions, equipped with M4A3E8 medium tanks and M26 Pershings, began arriving in the Pusan perimeter in early August and were rushed to the front to stem the North Korean advance. On 17 August 1950, a column from 107th Tank Regiment began an attack on defensive positions of the 1st Marine Provisional Brigade near Waegwan in the Naktong Bulge of the Pusan perimeter. The lead T-34 was hit by bazooka fire, without effect. On turning the corner, it came face-to-face with a Marine M26 Pershing at point-blank range. Having dominated US tanks in earlier battles, the overconfident North Koreans recklessly charged forward. The alert Marines beat the T-34s to the punch, firing two 90 mm rounds into the lead tank in quick succession, causing a catastrophic ammunition fire. The second tank was subjected to a hail of fire from recoilless rifles and bazookas, finally exploding when hit nearly simultaneously by two M26 Pershings. The third T-34 was pummelled in sim-

The most elementary of the T-34 based recovery vehicles was the T-34-T, which merely involved removing the turret and replacing it with a cover and a simple hatch. These were used for towing and other recovery tasks. Some of these conversions are still in service in former Warsaw Pact countries; this particular vehicle was photographed in 1990.

ilar fashion. The final T-34 retreated and was knocked out by UN aircraft. Suddenly, the once 'invincible' T-34-85 was now derided as the 'Caviar Can'. On the night of 27 August, the NKPA launched its last major tank attack. Charging down the 'Bowling Alley' near Tabu-dong, T-34-85s ran straight into entrenched infantry supported by Co. C, 73rd Tank Battalion with M26 Pershings. The NKPA attack was stopped in two days of fighting, losing 13 T-34-85 tanks and five SU-76M assault guns. With the Inchon landings on 16 September 1950, the

NKPA was outflanked and forced into a headlong retreat back north.

The heaviest tank-vs-tank battles of the Korean war took place from August to October 1950. There were hardly any encounters with North Korean armour after November 1950, and Chinese tanks never played an important role in the fighting. US tanks knocked out 97 T-34-85s, and claimed a further 18 as probables; on the debit side a total of 34 US tanks were knocked out by North Korean armour, of which 15 were competely destroyed. The T-34-85 was generally less able to resist tank fire than their US opponents. It could be penetrated by any of the US medium tanks, while it had difficulty penetrating the M26 or M46 tanks. A US inspection of knocked-out T-34-85s found that 75 per cent of its crews were killed when hit by tank fire, compared to only 18 per cent of US medium tanks hit by T-34 fire. This was due in part to the US practice of hitting a tank repeatedly until it burned so as to make certain that it was knocked-out. In general, the US consensus was that the T-34-85 was an excellent tank, but that the North Korean crews were not as well trained as their American counterparts. In terms of combat performance, the T-34-85 and the M4A3E8 were fairly evenly matched. Although the M4A3E8 had a smaller calibre gun, the widespread availability of HVAP ammunition made it quite capable of penetrating the T-34-85's

The most elaborate of the post-war recovery vehicles was the Czechoslovak VT-34. The large superstructure contained a winch and cable drum. This type was also used by the Polish Army in slightly modified form (CW-34) as seen here. (Janusz Magnuski)

Following the retirement of many T-34-85s in the 1960s the Polish Army's WITPiS converted some surplus chassis into the WPT-34 armoured evacuation tractor. This vehicle, currently preserved at the Polish Army Museum near Warsaw, has much of its specialised tools removed, providing a clearer view of the new superstructure.

armour. Likewise, the T-34-85 had no particular problem penetrating the armour of the M4A3E8 at normal combat ranges. In contrast, the M26 and M46 were a clear overmatch for the T-34-85. Both American tanks enjoyed thicker armour and

The T-34-85s built in Poland and Czechoslovakia in the early 1950s can be distinguished by their turret castings, which are noticeably smoother than Soviet examples. In addition, the shape of these turrets is also somewhat different. This Czechoslovak-manufactured T-34-85 went through the post-war rebuild, being refitted with a Czech Notek night driving lamp instead of the usual Soviet type. It served with the East German NVA, but was later donated to the Canadian tank museum at Camp Borden near Ottawa.

heavier firepower. In many respects the M26 and M46 were more comparable in size to the Soviet IS-2M Stalin heavy tank, rather than the T-34-85 medium tank.

Mid-East combat

Korea was to prove the last conflict in which the T-34-85 had a major impact. By the early 1950s, the T-54A was available in quantity, and the T-34-85 became increasingly obsolete. But in the 1950s and 60s, the T-34-85 was widely used in successive Mid-East conflicts. The rise of Arab nationalism turned Egypt, Syria, and Iraq against Britain and France, and towards the Soviet Union. In 1956, Egypt began receiving its first T-34-85s and SU-100s from a large order placed with the Czechoslovak government with Soviet approval. These arrived too late to see much fighting in the 1956 crisis, although Anglo-French forces did encounter a small number. At the same time, Syria began receiving T-34-85s directly from the USSR. By the time of the 1967 Six Day War, the T-34-85 was still used extensively by both Syria and Egypt, but front-line armoured units were already being equipped with new T-54As. Although the Egyptian 4th Armoured Division was still partly equipped with the T-34-85, most were in tank regiments supporting infantry forma-

The Polish Army followed the Soviet programme of modernising its T-34-85s in two stages, designated as T-34-85M1 and T-34-85M2. The T-34-85M2 conversion seen here was the most extensive undertaken within the Warsaw Pact, and included features to permit the tank to use a snorkel for deep wading. The snorkel can be seen fitted to the left hull side, and the gun mantlet is protected by a canvas water cover. This particular tank was locally manufactured at Labędy, with the characteristic smooth turret. (Janusz Magnuski)

tions. In total, Egypt lost 251 T-34-85s and 51 SU-100s in the debacle in the Sinai in 1967. Syria lost a much smaller number of T-34-85s defending the Golan Heights, as well as seven SU-100s. The Sinai was not the only theatre where Egyptian T-34-85s saw action. They were also deployed during Egypt's ill-fated intervention in the Yemen civil war in 1962-67; Yemeni T-34-85s took part in subsequent coups and civil wars between North Yemen (YAR) and South Yemen (PDRY). Egypt later received additional T-34-85s directly from the USSR, adding to their inventory of Czechoslovak T-34-85s.

By the time of the 1973 Yom Kippur War, T-34-85s had been withdrawn from most front-line units. The Syrians still had some in static defensive positions, but tank and mechanised units had converted almost entirely to the T-54, T-55 or T-62. The Syrian Army converted a portion of its T-34-85s into self-propelled guns by removing the turret and substituting a Soviet D-30 122 mm howitzer. The Egyptians followed suit in the late 1970s, mounting both the D-30 122 mm howitzer and the BS-3 100 mm field gun in an improvised turreted mounting.

Iraq began purchasing T-34-85s from the Soviet Union in 1959 along with T-54As. The T-34-85 was no longer in the front-line when the war with Iran broke out in 1980, but severe attrition forced some Iraqi armoured units to deploy these veterans in combat; most were rebuilt T-34-85 Model 1969 tanks. And during the savage fighting in Lebanon, several guerrilla factions employed the T-34-85; the PLO received about 60 tanks from Hungary.

Part of the 1969 modernisation programme was the addition of a new mounting at the rear of the tank for a 200-litre fuel drum. This example is Polish; the Soviet type usually had the stowage rack for the smoke canister located below and behind, rather than on top as seen here.

The T-34-85 in Asian conflicts

After the Korean War, the T-34-85 generally had a quiet time in the Asian-Pacific region. The NVA had a number of T-34-85 units during the Vietnam conflict but, due to their age, these saw little service. In the 1972 Quang Tri offensive, at least one T-34-85 regiment was committed to the fighting near the DMZ, but appears to have been wiped out by B-52 strikes. The South Vietnamese captured at least one T-34-85 modified into an improvised anti-aircraft vehicle by mounting Chinese Type 63 twin 37 mm guns in a crude open turret in place of the usual armament. Vietnam used T-34-85s in small numbers during its border war with China in February 1979, and at least one was captured, now resting in the army museum in Beijing. Finally, in the 1980s, T-34-85s were used extensively by the army of the Democratic Republic of Afghanistan in the civil war against the Mujihadeen. As often as not, these arthritic antiquities were used as static defence positions.

The T-34-85 in African conflicts

The last region where the T-34-85 remained viable was Africa. This was in no small measure due to the almost complete lack of tanks in sub-Saharan Africa until the 1970s, when many Marxist regimes were modernised with equipment donated by the Soviet Union. The Ethiopian army used the T-34-85 in its war with the Eritrean rebels, and the rebels in turn captured many and put them into action against their former masters. The T-34-85 was used in the Ethiopian-Somali clashes in 1977, and in the interminable fighting within Somalia. The Soviet Union began supplying the FAPLA (Angolan Army) with T-34-85 tanks in 1975, shortly after independence. These were blooded in clashes between the Marxist forces and Jonas Savimbi's rival UNITA forces in the autumn of 1975. At least one fell victim to a Panhard AML-90 supplied by Zaire and manned by South African advisers. In 1980-81, FAPLA T-34-85s were used to support the PLAN (People's Liberation Army of Namibia) during the fighting with South Africa over control of what was then called South-West Africa, and were first encountered in some numbers during Operation 'Protea' in 1981. At least two were destroyed in encounters with South African Defence Force (SADF) Ratel-90 armoured cars, and eight were captured. The T-34-85 was the mainstay of the Angolan and Cuban forces in their battles with the UNITA guerrillas and the South African Defence Forces in the early 1980s. But by the time of the big armoured battles in 1987, the venerable T-34s had been mostly replaced by Soviet-supplied T-55 and T-62 MBTs. The T-34-85 was adequate to deal with light infantry, but proved vulnerable when faced with better trained and

equipped forces, such as the South Africans in their versatile armoured cars. In the 1980s and 1990s, small numbers of T-34-85s were used by the FRELIMO guerrilla forces during the fighting with Rhodesian, and later Zimbabwean forces.

Combat in other regions

The T-34-85 saw combat in many far-flung corners of the globe. In 1956, Hungarian insurgent forces manned a few ex-Hungarian army T-34-85s in the hopeless fight against the invading Red Army. During Operation 'Attila', the Turkish intervention in Cyprus in August 1974, the Greek Cypriot National Guard resisted with a handful of T-34-85s provided by Yugoslavia. Following the break-up of Yugoslavia in the early 1990s, the remaining T-34-85s were split up amongst the combatants. The '85 has been widely used by the Bosnian Serb Army (BSA), often fitted with improvised appliqué armour.

The one region where the T-34-85 has seen little combat use is the Americas. Cuba began receiving some T-34-85s and SU-100s in the early 1960s, and a small number saw action against American-backed forces during the abortive Bay of Pigs invasion in April 1961. There were several small-scale engagements between rebel M41 light tanks and Cuban T-34-85s and SU-100s, M41 crews apparently winning the few tank duels that took place.

Yugoslavia planned to manufacture their own version of the T-34-85 as the **Teski Tenk Vozilo A** *(Heavy Tank Type A), in 1949. But only seven were built before the scheme collapsed. Although more streamlined, the Yugoslav version had less internal volume due to the new turret and the modified hull front. (Janusz Magnuski)*

THE PLATES

A1: *T-34-85 Model 1943, 38th Separate Tank Regiment, 53rd Army, Umansko-Botoshankskiy Operation, 29 March 1944*

This was one of the first T-34-85 units to see combat, and it was initially deployed in the winter of 1944 around the key road junction at Balta (Ukraine), near the Romanian border. On 15 March 1944, this regiment, commanded by Major Ivan A. Gorlach, was presented with 19 new T-34-85s and 21 OT-34 flamethrowers. The tanks were named *Dmitriy Donskoi* after the legendary Muscovite tsar (1359-1389), who vanquished the Tartars at Kulikovo in 1380. Funds to purchase the tanks were collected by the Russian Orthodox Church and Metropolitan Nikolai presented them at the 15 March 1944 hand-over ceremony. There have long been reports that some tanks funded by the church were painted with the Orthodox Cross, but no photographic evidence of this has survived.

The camouflage finish is a scruffy whitewash over the usual dark green.

A2: *T-34-85 Model 1945, 63rd Guards Tank Brigade, 10th Guards Tank Corps, Prague, May 1945*

The 10th 'Urals Volunteer' Guards Tank Corps began re-equipping with the T-34-85 in March 1944. This is the tank of Lt. I.G. Goncharenko, the first tank to enter Prague during the fighting in May 1945. Each of the three brigades in the corps used this geometric design, with the other two brigades using one (61st GTB) or two columns (62nd GTB) in the centre. Goncharenko's tank was knocked out by a Hetzer in the Prague fighting, and it was decided to honour his valour in suitable fashion. Unfortunately, the tank selected as Goncharenko's memorial was an IS-2m heavy tank, and his tank's numbers

Above: Two T-34-85 tanks of the North Korean 16th Armoured Brigade knocked out in fighting with US Marine Corps' M26 Pershings of the 1st Tank Battalion near Yongsan on 3-4 September 1950. Most of the tanks provided to the NKPA were manufactured in 1946. Both of these tanks have the common cast turret, and the nearer of the two is partly fitted with the cast spoke wheel. (USMC)

Below: Another T-34-85 of the 16th Armoured Brigade knocked out near Yongsan, probably by an air strike using napalm. This provides a good view of the composite cast turret with its flat rear turret floor. This particular example has the post-war split mushroom vents. (USMC)

were mistakenly depicted as 23, not 1-24. The memorial was the subject of a popular local legend, that the '23' on the tank was a prophecy: '1945+23=1968' – the year that Red Army tanks appeared again, this time to crush the Prague Spring. This IS-2 remained in place until the early 1990s, when a local anarchist group decided to paint it pink. The Russian government lodged an irate protest; the tank was repainted dark green. After it was painted pink a second time, the Czech government decided to remove it to the army museum rather than incur the wrath of the Russian embassy yet again.

A small number of the newly arrived Czechoslovak T-34-85 of the Egyptian Army were captured by Anglo-French troops during Operation 'Musketeer', the seizure of the Suez canal in 1956. The Czechoslovak tanks can be readily distinguished by the smooth turret casting, the unique headlight cover, and the armoured cover over the infantry signalling button barely evident under the external fuel canister in this photo.

B: *T-34-85 Model 1944, 55th Guards Tank Bde, 7th Guards Tank Corps, Berlin, April 1945*

This tank displays typical markings from the Berlin campaign. In March 1945, the Allies agreed to adopt common identification insignia designed to prevent 'own goals'; mistaking them for the enemy, Anglo-American fighter aircraft had been strafing Soviet columns in Yugoslavia. Red Army tanks were to be painted with a white band around the turret, and a cross on the turret roof. The tank carries the tactical number 36, and the name Suvorov after the famous 19th-century Russian general. The 7th Guards Tank Brigade employed a standard tactical marking on the tanks of its three tank brigades. This consisted of a circle within a circle. The brigades were then numbered sequentially with the numbers 1, 2, 3 inside the circle (54th Gds. Tank Bde. = 1; 55th Gds. Tank Bde. = 2; 56th Gds. Tank Bde. = 3). This crew painted the brigade number again on the outside of the circle for clearer identification. In the case of this tank, the circle insignia was repeated on the upper right side of the turret rear. The white cross in front of the tactical insignia may have been a mistaken interpretation of the

Israeli forces also captured a small number of the new Czechoslovak armoured vehicles during the 1956 war, in this case, an Egyptian SU-100 tank destroyer. An SU-100 captured by British forces in 1956 is currently preserved at the Bovington tank museum in the UK, while another captured by Israeli forces was sent to the US for technical evaluation and is now preserved at the Ordnance Museum at Aberdeen Proving Ground, Maryland. (Israeli Government Press Office)

A few of the T-34-85 tanks captured from the Egyptians in 1956 were repainted and briefly put into Israeli service, at least for the duration of a victory parade. So far as is known, the Israeli army never used the T-34-85 in combat. (Israeli Government Press Office)

instructions to paint the cross on the turret roof. In late April 1945, the Red Army captured a few German tanks with the white cross insignia in their sector. This discovery prompted a rethink, and on 29 April 1945 the identification order was rescinded in favour of painting a white triangle on all Red Army armoured vehicles as of 1 May 1945. But this later order was not widely followed.

C: *T-34-85 Model 1945, 6th Guards Tank Army, Grand Khingan Mountains, Manchuria, August 1945*

The Soviet assault on the Japanese Kwangtung Army in 1945 was heavily reinforced by tanks dispatched from the European theatre following the conclusion of the war with Germany. These units tended to follow the markings used by the Red Army from the spring 1945 campaign. In Manchuria, many tanks had a broad white band painted down the centre of the vehicle as an air identification marking. This was sometimes interrupted on the rear of the turret if a tactical number was present. This tank carries the typical Red Army three digit white tactical marking, and a white brigade insignia consisting of a bisected white circle; the specific brigade is not known.

D: *T-34-85 Model 1945, 105th Armoured Brigade, North Korean People's Army, Seoul, South Korea, July 1950*

The T-34-85 followed the internal layout of the earlier T-34s in most respects. The big difference

The arrival of T-34-85 tanks in Syria in the mid-1950s created some strange bedfellows. This Syrian armoured unit includes one of the German PzKpfw IV Ausf.Js obtained from Czechoslovakia and France in the late 1940s, along with an improvised armoured car based on a Canadian Otter.

The Peoples Army of Vietnam had a number of T-34-85 tanks in service during the Vietnam war, but they saw little combat. This unusual vehicle was a local conversion consisting of a Chinese Type 63 twin 37 mm anti-aircraft gun mounted in an improvised turret to create an air defence vehicle. It was captured by South Vietnamese troops in the 1972 Quang Tri offensive and shipped to the US for technical evaluation. It is currently preserved at the Ordnance Museum at Aberdeen Proving Ground, Maryland.

Czechoslovakia in the mid-1950s. These tanks have the characteristic Czechoslovak turret casting shape, the guard over the front headlights and the infantry signal fairing on the rear of the left hull side. Syrian vehicles were left in dark olive green, essentially the same colour as used by the Warsaw Pact at the time.

The air recognition symbol was a large white

was the enlarged three-man turret (gunner and commander on left, loader on right). In order to more effectively coordinate the crew, the radio was moved from the right hull front into the turret near the commander. The interior of the T-34-85 was painted gloss white, although many sub-components were left in their original finish, often dark green, black or completely unpainted. The engine compartment was generally exterior dark green, although many components were painted gloss black, or left in their original metallic finish.

E: T-34-85 Model 1953 (Czechoslovak production), 44th Armoured Brigade, Syrian Army, Ein Fite, Golan Heights, 10 June 1967

As in the case of the Egyptian Army, the Syrian Army made a large purchase of T-34-85 from

The Iraqi Army still had a number of T-34-85 tanks in use during the 1980-88 war with Iran. This particular example near Baghdad in 1982 is a T-34-85 Model 1969 based on a wartime 1944 production vehicle with the split commander's hatch. It is fitted with starfish wheels, but does not have the usual rear 200-litre fuel drum racks. It is camouflaged with swathes of olive drab over a sand-coloured base. (Leif Hellstrom)

Above: *During the war between Ethiopia and Somalia over the Ogaden in 1978, the T-34-85 was used by both sides. Here, Somali engineers repair a captured Ethiopian T-34-85 Model 1969 for use by the Western Somali Liberation Front. This vehicle has the full Model 1969 retrofit, including the rear fuel rack, the infra-red night driving equipment, and the external fuel pump. The turret is a post-war composite type with the split mushroom ventilators.*

circle with hollow centre. The Syrian practice was to name their tanks after martyrs (Al-Shaheed) of previous wars, usually from the 1948 fighting against Israel. This particular tank carries the name *Al Shaheed Hormuz Yunis Butrus* on the turret front.

There are two additional tactical insignia: a red triangle on either side of the turret and a coloured band. The colour of the band is not certain and although shown here as red, it may have been blue or green. The Syrian Army has traditionally used geometric shapes to distinguish units, although details of the system are not known to the authors.

A column of Somali T-34-85 Model 1969 tanks on parade in Mogadishu in the 1980s during the war with Ethiopia over the Ogaden. The insignia is a red over black square trimmed in pale blue with a white star on a pale blue disc in the centre. The national blue disc with white star insignia is repeated on the corners of the hull front.

The crew of a Somali T-34-85 Model 1969 pose for photographers at the time of the 1978 Somali-Ethiopian conflict. On this vehicle, only the red and black arm of service insignia is carried on the turret side, without the blue and white national insignia. Soviet intervention on the Ethiopian side, backed by Cuban troops, finally drove the Somali army out of Ethiopia.

The Angolan FAPLA and Cuban forces in Angola both used the T-34-85 in their battles with the South African Defence Forces in Namibia in the 1980s. This is an Angolan T-34-85 Model 1969 captured by the South Africans. It shows the full range of Model 1969 features: starfish wheels, infra-red driver's headlight, the external fuel pump box, repositioned MDSh racks on the hull side and rear fuel drum stowage racks.

F: *T-34-85 Model 1960 (Czechoslovak production), Al-Murabitun Lebanese Militia, Lebanese Civil War, Beirut, 1982*

This T-34-85 was turned over to one of the pro-Syrian Lebanese militia factions, the Al-Murabitun, during the vicious civil war in Beirut in the early 1980s. It is camouflaged in a rough pattern of medium brown over the usual dark green base colour. Besides the militia name on the turret side in black and white, the crew has also pasted on pictures of one of the militia leaders. These were not the only T-34-85s operating in Beirut at the time. In March 1981, the Palestinian Liberation Organisation was supplied with about 60 T-34-85s by Hungary, the first time the PLO had any significant number of tanks.

G1: *T-34 (122 mm D-30) Self-propelled Howitzer, Syrian Army, Golan Heights, 1973 Middle Eastern War*

In the late 1960s, Syrian arsenals converted a small number of T-34-85 tanks into self-propelled howitzers by removing the turret and substituting an exposed Soviet D-30 122 mm howitzer. The chassis used for these conversions was the standard Czechoslovak T-34-85. Additions included five ammunition stowage boxes on the hull sides,

and a small mounting for the gun which projected over the hull front. They were painted in the standard Syrian camouflage of the period, consisting of a base colour of dark green, with patches of light sand and medium brown. These vehicles saw combat service in the 1973 fighting on the Golan Heights, where at least one was captured.

G2: *T-122 122 mm Self-propelled Howitzer, Egyptian Army, 1980*

In the late 1970s, the Egyptian Army's Abu-Zaabal Engineering Industries Plant No. 100 in Alyubiyah province embarked on a programme to mechanise a portions of the Egyptian artillery force using outdated T-34-85 Model 1969 tanks. The roof and aft portions of the turrets were cut away, and an enlarged turret made of sheet armour was reconstructed around the remains of the old turret. Two different gun mountings were developed, one for the Soviet D-30 122 mm howitzer as seen here and one for the BS-3 Model 1944 100 mm field gun. The D-30 variant was sometimes called T-34/122 or T-122. The total production run of these vehicles is not known but was probably a few dozen. The vehicles were painted in a pale sand colour with large spray-painted patches of medium field drab.

INDEX

(References to illustrations are shown in **bold**. Plates are prefixed 'pl.' with commentary locators in brackets, e.g. 'pl. **D** (44-45)'.)

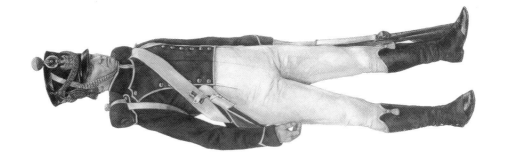 

OSPREY PUBLISHING

FIND OUT MORE ABOUT OSPREY

❑ Please send me the latest listing of Osprey's publications

❑ I would like to subscribe to Osprey's e-mail newsletter

Title/rank

Name

Address

Postcode/zip   state/country

e-mail

I am interested in:

❑ Ancient world
❑ Medieval world
❑ 16th century
❑ 17th century
❑ 18th century
❑ Napoleonic
❑ 19th century

❑ American Civil War
❑ World War I
❑ World War II
❑ Modern warfare
❑ Military aviation
❑ Naval warfare

Please send to:

USA & Canada:
Osprey Direct USA, c/o MBI Publishing, P.O. Box 1,
729 Prospect Avenue, Osceola, WI 54020

UK, Europe and rest of world:
Osprey Direct UK, P.O. Box 140, Wellingborough,
Northants, NN8 2FA, United Kingdom

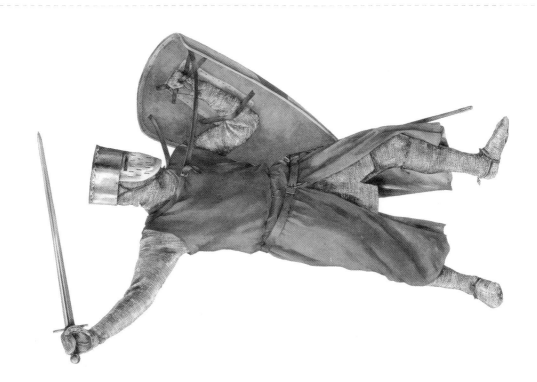

OSPREY
PUBLISHING

www.ospreypublishing.com

call our telephone hotline
for a free information pack

USA & Canada: 1-800-826-6600
UK, Europe and rest of world call:
+44 (0) 1933 443 863

Young Guardsman
Figure taken from *Warrior 22:
Imperial Guardsman 1799–1815*
Published by Osprey
Illustrated by Richard Hook

Knight, c.1190
Figure taken from *Warrior 1: Norman Knight 950 – 1204 AD*
Published by Osprey
Illustrated by Christa Hook

POSTCARD